Language for the
Living and the Dead

Language for the
Living and the Dead

Poems

CHRIS RANSICK

A Division of Samizdat Publishing Group

CONUNDRUM PRESS A Division of Samizdat Publishing Group.
PO Box 1279, Golden, Colorado 80402

For information, email info@conundrum-press.com.

ISBN: 978-1-9386331-5-7

Library of Congress Cataloging-in-Publication Data is available upon request.

Conundrum Press books may be purchased with bulk discounts for educational, business, or sales promotional use. For information please email: info@conundrum-press.com

Conundrum Press online: conundrum-press.com
Book Design: Sonya Unrein

Poems from this collection, in present or previous versions, have appeared in the following publications:

"Parenting on Pluto" *Cincinnati Review*; "The Wounding Moment," "194 Things to Do," and "The Morning of My Release" *Pilgrimage*; "What the Knife Revealed" *Ars Medica*; "The Antikythera Mechanism" *Notre Dame Review*; "Paris Conundrum" *Prairie Schooner*; "A Screwball Rispetto" *Marginalia*; "When the Buzzards Return to Crestone" *Sycamore Review*; "The Scars of Gillette, Wyoming" *Many Mountains Moving*.

"Tango Villanelle" was part of the collaborative project *Love: A Joint Venture*, performed by Ballet Nouveau Colorado in 2010.

for Judy

Regardless of our dialect, we speak with the words of the dead.

—Robert Pogue Harrison

*But when we are searching for an example of what we
no longer have, we see it everywhere.*

—Michael Ondaatje

Contents

Parenting on Pluto

We two were once a planet, secure
in orbit around our sun, entitled in texts and

circled by moons whose dusty faces
stared at only us through the perpetual

Plutonian winter as though the universe
weren't a black beckoning beyond.

Science has banished us from the roll
but we still rotate and revolve,

sure nothing has changed, and everything.
Dwarfs now, aware of eons and asteroids

that will mark us and pock us and
finally knock us off all charts, leaving

just the old models in museums no one
visits. This edge of the solar system

has always been lonely and we had just a
brief reprieve between discovery and

exile, a short span of years when the people
were aware and named us for gods.

Now that blue rock streaks away
on its own trajectory toward collisions

we can imagine or remember distantly,
thumbing the scars of our own,

the craters and gullies on our chilled
crust, the contours invisible from afar.

The Antikythera Mechanism

Two thousand years on the seabed
fused elegant gears and dials, seized

planets mid-flight across a bronze plane.
Sphere-music halted with a last note

pealing out across the Aegean.
A sponge diver saw you shining there,

corroded wheels glinting in the murk
and silt swirling in ribs of a Roman ship,

fragments scattered by millennia of
current, cogs separated from cogs.

What workshop, what tools, what hands
rendered imagination and

observation into so fine a thing?
Your flaking metals tantalize the best

minds, hinting at astronomy and
lost insights, mysteries of celestial

motion, history of harvest and
planting and harvest again.

The lab-coated archeologist plumbs
your surfaces and guts with microfocus

tomography, capturing inscriptions
and hidden functions, the subtle oval

that lets the moon slip forward faster.
Venus, Mars, Mercury appear,

Jupiter and Saturn, an orrery
displaying the known universe.

Did the drowning astronomer gasp
for himself or because he knew

you would sink with him, burying
secrets so long in the teasing out?

What the Knife Revealed

I lay there on the table, a red beet ready for slicing but
dark blood, more purple than imagination,

would ooze only after I'd shut my eyes, little poisons
meant to soothe me doing well their work. The surgeon,

head chef of the meal of me, marked which tissues
to tear away, which to leave tattered, which to ignore

until next time. Then, with a steady hand, he slashed
a sharp blade, incising and spreading, venturing into

an interior where no suns penetrate, no breeze ever
blew through shaded fronds. I can't be sure but

something like memory tells me wild beasts, sheltered
all these years in that deep wood, leaped to my

defense, but as beings insubstantial, their fierce visages
were lost on the masked man. How they wailed

as they were cut down, one by one, to fall among
steel basins and gauzy beds. Nor were the birds of my

inspiration, raptors and singers, carrion eaters,
able to see the interloper, camouflaged in the murk.

Doctor, now spelunker in my cave of gristle and throb,
lit his head lamp and plunged down passages

too narrow for mere mortals, exposing graffiti
left by ancient prisoners in those soft cells.

The orchestra played on, bass drum heart, wind section
wheezing under the influence, the piccolo run of

synapses firing, the cello strings roiling in the gut.
So it was he must come, at last, to the vein of black rock,

bespattered with flecks of bright ore, once rising magma
but now held fast in the crevasses where flow ceased.

Animal, vegetable, mineral—I've always known
this is all we are, but mirrors suggest another self and

so many commercials and priests insist there's more,
it's hard to resist the material tug, the promise of

awakening from anesthesia with wings and a good view
forever. When I did wake, there was only a small

window in a pale green wall, looking out over a
parking lot. The nurses were nice but not angels.

When the Blind Woman Steps from the Curb

Everything stops, magpies stalking
across grass, cumulus bulging
above prairie, falling gold
cottonwood leaves, the breeze,
the car, your heart. Everything

stops except your brain that blurts stop
the car. Suspended thus, pilot steering
a fast machine about to deliver
injury, you relinquish the monsters
you harbor and have come to love.

Strands of black hair frame her
placid face. Her lips move but you hear
nothing in the frozen moment as she
advances, the only animate being. She taps
pavement with her long white cane,

a miner emerging into brilliant sun
after a season among dark stone glades.
Brake lights multiply, red stars
coalescing. Will the bus turn the corner
and crush her when motion resumes?

You, too, are blind to your death,
groping your way toward that future.
Whatever happens here, you will
pay better attention and never step
sightless from a curb into eternity.

Then a stranger risks her own
fragile bones, dashes and seizes
the woman's elbow, yanks her backward,
almost vicious. The whole scene
rushes to action, squealing brakes,

some idiot's horn, the inaudible
pumping of adrenal glands, the suck
of uptaken breath, and she slips past
on your right, missed by inches,
safe and seared into memory.

The Wounding Moment

Don't try to tell me now
we were otherwise kind to the girl.
Such lies mock both the truth and
what we've become since with our
accumulated years. I know I will walk
backward through nightmares forever,
trying but unable to catch her tears
in my outstretched palm.
When you tormented her that day
at the woods' edge, summer sky
stormed because your words
curdled clouds. Yes, she was fat,
her skin raw with blemishes.
I flinched when she raised her head,
red-rimmed eyes fierce, and learned
from her how to speak none of it.
I was, as always, captive in my
little-brotherness to you, my captain,
but I disowned you there with the
sunlight glinting off your blond hair,
all your beauty still somehow less
than her anger, sheathed.

The Nightmares of My Sisters

When you thrash through a bramble patch
of troubled sleep, thorns tearing flesh,
slick slope tricking heels to stumble,

and though this fearful flight occurs
in your beds in Seattle, Poughkeepsie, El Paso,
know I am your partner, lashed

to my own berth beneath dark peaks
that each night cheat sinking sun. Your animus
my anima, your incubus my

succubus, hovering above thin sheets,
not quite a shape, just a shadow, cold
smoke, toxic erotic clergy of dreams.

Wake, sisters, wake, release that panic
pursuing you down some forest path
where the pines rustle and shudder

as you pass. Rise whether day has come
or is still far off. Step to the threshold
of your home and sip fresh air,

let oxygen trickle through arteries,
chase the residue of trepidation
out the ends of your long lovely hair.

Ataraxia

On a stone couch beneath a branch
heavy hung with wind-polished apples,

the old philosopher opened his
third eye, the one only masters own.

Crow was somewhere cawing of snow
in the foothills falling, mutable skies

teasing the tree and his flesh at once
sun-warmed and breeze-chilled.

Scents adrift entered him, brown leaf
and moist soil, perfume of ripe grapes

pendulous in shade, all their juices
promises to be honored in the mouth.

Melodies soft-surging from every
plane mixed silky wine into memory and

his tongue could taste her again
though she was gone, his hand could

trace her shape in the air, pausing
then swimming again among

ghost tresses almost auburn almost
fragrant and so never forever.

Paris Conundrum

I saw your shimmering tower
and your dirty gutters, dogshit

at the entrance
to the fancy brasserie,

women in sunglasses and silk scarves
walking rapidly past a kneeling

immigrant with cardboard sign:
j'ai faim

I heard buskers on the steps
of Sacré Coeur

butchering already bad
American pop songs

but also the violinist
running Vivaldi's arpeggios

as sunset blazed bright
through the windows of Sainte-Chapelle,

casting liquid light
across listeners' skin.

I drank your hundred-Euro wines
and tiny cups of black coffee

I walked wide boulevards between
boutiques of chrome and glass,

I walked narrow bent lanes where
hucksters loitered among middens

of shattered plates. I was cursed
by a cheap artist in Montmartre

and listened at the graves of
Sartre and Wilde for some last

wise remark, but only the crows
had something to say

and I speak neither French
nor the language of caws.

I stood by the Romans'
tepidarium at Cluny

counting the layers of mortar
and brick and mortar again.

I wandered Notre Dame's
vaulted aisles while

ethereal voices sang out
on Good Friday the

suffering song, penitents
kneeling to kiss a reliquary.

I walked along the Seine
and saw Hemingway's ghost

chasing down pigeons in the
Luxembourg gardens,

hungry as only a
dead novelist can be,

and in a station of the Metro
there were no petals on a

wet, black bough, only
faces of tired tourists

and a French wife berating
her bored husband in his

black beret. Finally,
it was time to leave.

The train ran its gauntlet of
graffitied walls between

broken-down houses,
small plots planted for

spring with
greens and onions.

At the airport I was
frisked by a rubber-gloved man,

the only person in France
who touched me.

How to Feed a Writer

Tempt the tongue with husky whispers the ears
barely hear but the belly remembers.
Place marinated steak on the embers.
Disregard his impatience. Ignore tears
borrowed from the protagonist, page eight.
Serve first for thirst the chilled and peppered booze
and let her stand beneath blue dragonflies
as soft winds blow lindens and day grows late.
Feed a writer everything delicious,
nothing bitter as novels to finish,
old poems to varnish, memoirs to banish.
What they curse and scribe, be it auspicious
or doomed or blamed on their big busy heads,
will be but words when they lie in their beds.

Gallina Stargazer, 1275

Unburied, you gazed at the whirling sky
above, one last sunset, one last night of

brilliant stars. Tell us, does the soul depart
upward into black, toward such spheres,

or does it leak into soil and join the mother,
a different darkness, a comforting heat?

Now pale people pick through your ribs,
brush red sand from empty eye sockets,

soon to release you from that forever gaze.
They say it was a swift attack, a massacre

over in minutes, your man and babe
bludgeoned into the dirt beside you,

a whole village vanishing, meager corn
still on the metate, water in the olla.

To your attackers you were the witch
who brought drought, dried the spring

to a seep, turned the cornfields from loam
into desolate plains of cracked mud

penetrated by stunted stalks under fierce
summer sun. Fear was the only surplus then,

vented but never banished by violence.
So you lie a while longer, once again staring

into eternity, wind to caress your bones and
sing in the canyon a familiar song.

A Screwball Rispetto

Your target—his hands clenching the bat.
Grip the ball with a falcon's claw and roll
over the top as you release, snapping that
red seam down into the plate's black hole.

Heat it hard so the pitch comes fast
and a bit wild, inside middle so it breaks
in toward tender knuckles as he takes
a stuttering stride and swings right past.

The Comedian Takes His Own Life

One March afternoon, just when chill
crept back into weak sun-warmed nooks,
he greeted me on the stairs, half-smile
he always wore, ambling gait from an old
wound. He said, "Hey, how's it going?"
but not like goodbye, more like he
really wanted to know. We stepped onto
the patio and he lit a cigarette, moving aside,
aware of the wind. We were friends
in that natural way of two men who know
how deeply fucked the whole thing is
and yet there's something to share,
though I couldn't tell you, then or now,
just whom he loved, or whether anyone,
or where he'd go if he had but a week to live,
which he did. I didn't know that, either.
There was nothing funny in the conversation.
He never laughed—just a sneer when
stupid people did stupid things and we'd
look at each other, *knowing*. So I told him
a problem I was having and he listened,
petty but I complained anyway, and now,
looking back, I regret that most of all.
How could I know in a matter of days he'd
loop a length of climbing rope over a door
and tie the end around his throat,
slow-strangling in the gloom, alone?
If I could I'd go back to that moment
where we stood in the spring damp,
wind ruffling our hair, smoke swirling.
I'd slap myself until I shut up, I'd
lean across and hug him and whisper
in his ear, it's okay it's okay it's okay.

If You Had Such Wings

If you had such wings, then where?
Soar, circle, dive, hover,
come back down to Earth from the air.

Does a body dream better up there?
Imagine the wind as your lover.
If you had such wings, then where?

Fly away and until you're aware
the horizon is all we discover.
Come back down to Earth from the air.

Come back to the bed you share.
A gift means the most to the giver.
If you had such wings, then where?

At the table, your empty chair
can wait for you forever.
Come back down to Earth from the air.

Live as you are, if you dare.
Let your feet know the ground you cover.
If you had such wings, then where?
Come back down to Earth from the air.

Eternity, Colorado

for Scott

White canoe props up a brown garage,
glyphs gouged and scored along its hull by
unseen river rocks, gravelly shallows.

Paint peels slowly from a shuttered store's
door in a blue wall, windows grimed with their
long view forever of the ghost café, a gauntlet of

derelict dwellings hot summer sun
illuminates. Eternity's grain elevator marks
the silent town's terminus where wind polishes

a leaning green barn, never again
a shelter, only a bleached canvas absorbing
starlight from deep space. Cottonwoods paint

live shadows on pavement, splash the flanks
of a roan mare standing asleep in a field
of shortgrass, a forgotten farm tacked to earth by

twin rusted laundryline Ts dumb-gesturing
ignorance beside two stuck trucks and a
cinderblock shelter tagged with fading graffiti.

Cooking Lessons

1

Break the egg carefully.
Not the world, though. Eat that
by the rough spoonful.

2

Forget where you come from,
familiar flavors in your mouth.
Watch blue flame pass through
steel to simmer broth.

On the counter rises dough
so soft some may doubt its
very existence beyond this
kitchen in Provence.

The roux must not be rushed.
Stir and remember long journeys,
silent departures from
dim terminals. Do not

rush the roux. Take time
to witness gold infuse the sauce.
Refill friends' glasses with
laughter and juiced rubies.

3

The server brings
a warm baguette
to your sidewalk table and
every sadness leaves as
lights along Rue St. Michel
reveal themselves magic lights.

Yes that's the right wine and yes
to the long walk home and finally
yes to whatever else.

Muddy Stream

This is the muddy stream where the poor child
drowned, late August, loud crows wild
in the maples, wings black against sky red.
That night, his parents lay down in their bed
and both dreamed a dream of an endless field

he walked into, waving. Breeze mild
through hay-colored hair through goldenrod spilled
and ghost gown trailing, toward the far wood fled.
This is the muddy stream

that turns a wheel where sorrows are milled
in a village where everyone's mouth is filled.
Come, I'll show you the mark in the mud
where his sneakers slid, rock that bruised his head,
water that enfolded him, calm, beguiled.
This is the muddy stream.

Sick Wife

Winged Victory, missing her head, yet commands
the Louvre staircase, proud breasts thrust out
over lost waves, long gone sea breeze catching

stone gown's folds that cling to majestic
armless femininity, proof decay breaks down
even carved marble, aloof from viruses, from

free radicals, from macular degeneration and
all nature of cruel aging. Small female, large planet
full of illness, miracle body made with flaws.

The hot soup helped but not enough. Rest, rest,
let macrophages eat away invaders.
All errands will wait another day, all undone

tasks will stay stacked, and needy spawn
will know to need you still come blue-lit
dawn, those mouths that can never be filled.

Wrestle consciousness down into the murk
sleep spreads round, be weary this once
without excuse, surrender unconditionally,

you who so rarely capitulate, rebel-in-the-hills
who will not relinquish her rusty gun.
The doors are locked, the dog is snug, cold wind

cannot penetrate this house. If when ancient
you find yourself alone and ill, remember us
resilient and young, side by side until we fell.

Tango Villanelle

I move toward you into a dark
where a blue flame burns on a desert plain.
I move from you but I must come back

again to your hair, a swarm of birds so black
in flight round your face, a wild skein.
I move toward you into a dark

opaque as coal, incense smoke
rising from your gown's red terrain.
I move from you but I must come back,

searching amid forest dusk, the murk
fragrant with spice of autumn rain.
I move toward you into a dark

where I am lost, a distant spark
fading in twilight's shadow refrain.
I move from you but I must come back

inside your gyre where passion's torque
spins me until all my pleasure is pain.
I move toward you into a dark.
I move from you though forever I come back.

When the Buzzards Return to Crestone

We'd spooked a dozen dark cruisers
off perches in a cottonwood copse
ablaze with gold leaves, and they rose

prehistoric mad black, a flapping
racket ruining the creekgully quiet
and he said, *Capistrano can*

keep its swallows. I'll take this flock of
turkey vultures any day. He couldn't say
what brought them back to this drainage

off Sangre de Cristo slopes, maybe
roadkill on Hwy 17, though guts
lie smeared on many other roads.

I know it's spring when they return, he said,
as the carrion craft circled the grove
and one by one settled again on

limbs thick enough to hold them,
their ugly beautiful bald heads red
in October sun. *They'll leave soon enough*

and that means winter on the way.
Nobody ever writes poems for vultures
except to curse them or render them

symbols of wretched death awaiting.
Winged hyenas, scavengers, call them
any pejorative term but remember

they can fly and you cannot, they
clean up the mess your car leaves behind,
they see their mates as lovely in the trees.

Casa, Del Norte

Dry wind burnishes elm tree's burls,
weathered paint the hot sun curls.

A hundred hammered nails hold fast
the slats of pine that they outlast,

the wood itself now giving way
to another night, another day.

Tall grass invades the welcome mat,
pierces the porch where Grandfather sat

cursing the drought, cursing the rain,
cursing the tracks that bore no train

until even the magpies, even the crows
abandoned his stunted cornfield rows

and flew away from forsaken dirt,
from the old clothesline where a tattered shirt

dangles down discolored shreds,
ghost scent sifting from the threads.

No one inhabits this house now,
rust on the doorknob, rust on the plow,

dust in the cupboards, flies on the sills,
last residents still beneath their hills,

dreaming the dreams of the ancient dead,
where the river is honey and the rocks are bread.

The Laughing Man

Maybe you'll meet him on a high cliff
or under a pier buttered with seafoam.

He may dance and cackle
at catastrophes aflame behind you

or create one more before your eyes.
Whatever you do, don't do what he says.

Don't laugh at the loneliest joke ever told,
no matter how the old fellow grins when

repeating the judge's harsh ruling,
voice shrill as wind through a crack.

He laughs at his despair and yours
since they're one and we all have to share.

He chortles and calls down shadows to seize
and infuse that part of you that knows

how canyon wrens wrestle mid-flight,
desperate to finish because they are falling.

Requiem for Dopamine

Dweller in dark synapses of
substantia nigra, liquid executive
hunkered in prefrontal cortex,

what will control the worst impulses
now that you will not come?
Eyes see but the mind does not

notice the furious wasp
poised to attack. The sting
and swelling flesh are but

abstractions, the pain a nuisance,
no reason to react.
Amid the amygdala fears sprawl

in a mandala of tremulous
memory and absent chemicals fail to
paint panic on a bleached grid,

amp a dead battery that can't
light the lamp. The body awaits
stimulation, muscles softening.

When will the neurons fire again,
spill quicksilver and awaken
the slumbering centaur?

In this desert, serotonin will not
compensate, busy with guts,
a bipolar miser content to tweak moods.

Mind muzzled, a starved man
will not recognize his last chance
and move from the cage's corner

to retrieve the slice of cherry pie
steaming, delicious, within reach.
The schizophrenic understands,

as does the addict whose engine
will not engage. Give us the right
pill and we will resume swimming

toward death, smiling despite
our knowledge of it, sparked by
tiny fish nibbling at our toes.

What the Boy I Was Tells the Man I Am

Don't look for me in the
wrecked, blessed woods.
I am not hiding among
blackberries and lemon balm,
nor in hip-deep snow under
bare maples. I am not crouched
in the split boulder's gap, feet
creek-muddied. Crows
caw about my ghost below
but their black tongues lie.

This kingdom once belonged to
an army of boys marching
in the sun. Their castle of sticks
collapsed, the last hostage a prince
released once he forgot
his desire for dirt. If you seek
artifacts, go dig your trenches.
You'll find no bones, no ruins,
just gossamer heat veiling faces,
warm breezes chasing faint voices.

I kissed that girl, not you.
October twilight traced our shapes
and yes, you remember, her lips
trembled. She since gave herself to
angry men, never again tender.
The boy you beat to tears on the grass
forgave you, though you have not
forgiven yourself. When will you open
the bars of your chest and set free
the blackbird you could not save?

That sad young nun finally fled,
she who leaned against her oak desk,
softly weeping in the stifling room.
One night she knelt and prayed in her cell
laid out a crucifix of onyx beads
on the narrow bed's white sheet,
gathered her garments in a paper sack
but left the black habit puddled
on the floor, walked away toward
a place no priest could find.

Don't come looking for me now.
The scar on your brow proves your
legendary fall from the tall pear tree.
Your bad shoulder aches from
too many screwballs, a decade hefting
newspaper bags. Your brothers, now
old men, have left no children here.
It's enough you still love crickets'
late summer songs, bright carp in ponds,
and sleek garter snakes in deep grass.

Twelve Things About a Banjolele

handmade Kalamazoo 1925

maple ebony calfskin steel

midwinter tones ride old riverblues

I am Catfish John I'm a prodigal son

long time gone since grandfather strummed

silent decades a wall decoration

17 frets on the pearwood neck

lithe tones burnish live woodgrain

old leather strap fits over a shoulder

learn here an intricate hybrid tongue

tell kids a kind spirit hides inside

music as heaven as water as lift

Scenes From a Miserable Week

1

There are things the body teaches
cruelly, taskmaster with its million nerves
made to transmit a rich palette of
colored pains, raw reds, a deep blue throb,
a yellow caul covering an anxious mouth.
Should you imagine you are a prince,
your body will chortle and ball you up
like a foil man, steal your sleep
until mad creatures jig at the margin of vision,
jangling limbs in their clown suits, grimaces
showing the teeth that gnaw you.

2

The young doctor called me *Dude.*
I simply wasn't ready for that, felt myself
slip into a bad place though I know
he meant it as comfort, camaraderie,
a sign he understood precisely how my
wracked flesh became thus wracked,
and knew to expect this of his flesh, too.

3

I confessed my sins to the woman with the
clipboard and stack of forms, though
some secrets she'd never learn, even if her
fingers fumbled through every soft organ
in my gut. She was just doing her job.
Then the man with the long needle ran
icy liquids into my arm and sirens sang
from rocky outcrops behind the curtains.
They whisked me down halls so clean
I wanted to weep, past waiting rooms, past
tilted tombstones beside mounded earth,
into a bright surgery. Shiny steel implements

meant for my skin served to remind
how vulnerable is flesh, how easily cut
from its mooring the heart. Were the faces
innocent or cruel behind their masks?
A hand swabbed my throat and I wondered
how much blood a body holds. I wanted sutures
before the scalpel ever sliced. Then I saw a
pale angel trembling in the corner
and from somewhere—accordion music?
There was no longer any doubt, I was slipping
and they would do what they must, what I'd
paid them to do. I'd wake up sore and
missing tissue, cured and sewn together.
And the last thing I saw was

4
In the worst moments, just after
panic subsides, one recalls health
as a distant, exotic country
washed by morning rain, wind pushing
sailboats over a bay, sun, oh yes,
that beautiful light and warmth
on the flesh of the world.
And there is red wine in the mouth
mingling with laughter and the
many names of love, the aroma of
warm, crusty bread, and caresses
calling the body to heal.

5
The lover becomes the nurse,
and passion, compassion.

6

Woman on the canyon's far cliff,
this is the place where one of us
will leave the other some cold dawn.
But not today. Let us begin again
the arduous descent down worn paths
shedding empty tasks, dry leaves
falling behind us. We will meet
midstream in that green river
that heals and sweeps us away,
embracing, each the receiver, humbled.

7

Body mine, you purged your poisons,
painted stellate shapes on my pillow.
I said things in delirium I wish I had
written down, pure poems heard only
by the cat, my failed amanuensis.

Body mine, I re-inhabit you with
greater reverence, never again to ignore
complex fluidity as though its source
were a permanent spring.
Give me a home again and forgive
the tyrant who gloated from his throne.
I have learned my nerves' capacities,
and the lessons sleepless nights teach.

Picking Apples in the Dark

Language breaks when I try to name
how your hand moves among shadows,
among moonwaxed leaves.

Pale globes wobble as the ladder
bends a glossy branch and you lean
into wind in your fiftieth autumn,

a land we no longer deny. I would
pick apples with you on our last day
and be filled up and be satisfied.

I Visited My House

I visited my house long after death,
home where I slept fifty thousand nights

in a basement room, place where I learned
the growth of grass, the health of dirt,

the shape of trees' shade, the slant of
solstice sun through the drapes, the scent

of the neighbor's towering lilacs, the sound
of his daughter who tortured pianos.

I visited my house where I no longer lived,
got down on my knees at the garden's edge,

paused at the unwatered strawberry patch,
dead mint still fragrant, wild thyme

scraggly but hanging on. I moved through rooms
where I once reclined, each silent

and reconfigured, unfamiliar furniture,
the aroma of strangers' meals in the air.

They'd painted the walls, they'd driven in nails,
hung a poster of a pop star where once

was a flower from Georgia O'Keefe.
I found them asleep and I hovered above

but the malice I felt dissipated because
I could tell that they loved in the house

where I'd lived, in a bed where we'd loved
in the bed that we had. It comforted me

that the lock on the door was the same sticky one
that had been there before. If I'd had my key

I could open it still, though incorporeal,
I've no need for a door. I shall never return

to my old house again for there's nothing to say
that has not yet been uttered by some other dead

disappointed home-haunter. All my children are gone,
though their cries linger on in the walls and halls,

where I nurtured their bodies and added the fuel
to the lamps of their souls until flames were sufficient

to burn on their own. Bless this house, bless this house,
let the new guest grow old here, salting its floors

with honest tears, scenting rooms with the blooms
of his dreams, singing out the sounds of his names.

Raven Complains, North Slope of Sopris

Dawn doesn't light the big couloir
until wind has its way,
lifts the last powder scarf off the
high cornice, polishes the meadow
to shine in hard April sun.
I fly faster than bear runs
but I'm black and night is through.
I can wait for breakfast until
lion finishes with old elk's carcass
but spring comes so slow it bores
even the talus tumbled under
the skirts of scrub oak.
So I'll wheel and caw my
one joke until someone, anyone,
laughs, until my throat opens
and shapes me a new note.

Street of Lost Companions

I wished your disease would be gone
and it was, a devil fleeing flesh
in a clatter of hooves and scales,
leaving behind a foul cloud.

What remained—man estranged from me
these many years, recognizable by the
mask of pain, map of murky tattoos.
A wild man, a howling anchorite

I embraced and who bit my cheek.
The blood ran black and up, into skies
that should have been blue, where the past
resides in rills and whorls far from any

planets. Once, when we were close,
bruised brothers, mere boys, you
fished from the Pacific
a wretched merman who couldn't swim.

I wished your disease would be gone
but there was no well, no stair to step
backward up, no lamp to rub, no dream
to blame, no hymn, no incantation

that would summon the slim young man
of memory. In truth, you remain
ensconced in your room, a prisoner
frightened by sunlight and unfamiliar music,

a priest of lonely liturgies, sealed inside
refractions, long corridors that emanate
from before and point toward narrow
tomorrows, where no light can escape.

Betrayal, Dupont Circle

You passed him first en route to lunch
where he squatted in an alcove, listless,
jangling despair in a wet paper cup.

Morning rain painted him into puddles,
melted the natural dignity of a man
as the coins against the cup whispered

povertypovertypovertypoverty
slithering past monuments and museums,
great Doric columns, Georgian revivals,

smoky-glass limos and gutter litter.
You knew that hunger, not in the body
but as the noumenal mind does,

a condition observable in nature, an
emblem of lack, a status achieved
by continual loss. All of this

rattled in your cranium while you
ingested expensive comestibles
leached of their panoply of flavors.

When you approached again the perch
where he crouched in drizzle, his eyes
poured past your pathetic defense

as muddy floodwater tops a weak dam,
mocking not with arrogance but rather
with betrayal, one animal of another.

A Friend Stops By to Say She's Dead

Not now, but on some morning
yet to come, sun on her hair speaking

mysteries and comfort with a stilled
tongue of light, she'll say her goodbye.

The body, only the body can answer
the last breaths true friends take.

Language grows useless approaching
the bed, whether a loved one lives

yet in her scented, warm limbs or
just disappeared there, estranged

beyond reunion. Remember the day
when you first trusted and spoke

without art of darkness. She
shivered but did not flee when you

cursed demons, grinned and added
her own black verses, made you feel

less alone, which cannot last,
which is what she came to say.

194 Things to Do

First, decipher directions
on the human body,
intricate charts and diagrams,
the loci of muscles and
nerves, the shy imagination.
Push, pull, flex, measure,
then leap as far as you can.
Your next task: take a splinter
from a small child's finger.
Remove it fast, before
serious tears, and soothingly
promise world peace.
Blackbirds sleep in the
pages of books; release them
at night so pursuers dash
toward darkness,
knowing nothing. Humbly
enter the garden and gather
ripe chilies so blazing hot
the French chef's knife goes soft.
Tell all the people who have
hurt you that you forgive
only fools, so they need
have no fear. Never explain
how the cogs of your millwheel
mesh, nor name the beast,
gentle and dumb, that
lowers its shoulders for the yoke.
When an old friend arrives,
sugar the evening with your
best wine, tales worth telling,
fists full of poems. Say nothing
of anger, or if you must,
speak of it in your sleep.

Put down those rocks and they
turn into rockets, put down
that pen and let a ghost
take it up, his ciphers echoes
of lost language meant for the
living and the dead.
Enter your house humbly and
embrace your woman, say
love never stops murmuring
her names in your ear.
Listen more than you speak
and meadows will bloom from
confusion and mud. Stop bleeding
already and clear your calendar.
Your list is shorter now. Lower
your head and work.

Does the Bear Own Roger?

Does the bear own Roger or Roger the bear?
Are any of us anywhere
near the right place? Who owns what
when where? My money is on the bear

because it's the prisoner whose cage
is a shrinking wild place, ruined lodgepole
for bars, a swollen tributary for a
natural boundary. But Roger owns

wisdom, that ability to see through
the trees the elusive peace. He won't
admit it but Lorca makes him shiver
and the bear will never read

"Romance Sonambulo" and Roger will
nevermore sleep in a cave.
Morning light found them staring
into each other, full of recognition.

Make of that what you will. The bear
did own Roger but gave him back
himself, which was the greatest gift,
which changes everything.

Cahirballykinvarga

Goat gods atop remote rocks,
this is your village now.

Ghostsmoke from turf fires
sifts from the taciturn farmer's

chimney, scenting the ruins.
The moss is ochre, the May grass

green enough to make eyes ache.
Even to look at your horn's arc hurts.

Leaves of blooming hawthorn hush
children who haunt by running

the rain-slick chevaux-de-frise,
laughter spilled over tilted karst.

What good is the past to goats, to
men who don't last, whose lust

is enough, whose walls fall
from wind and wind plus time?

A Man, a Fire, a Dog

Thirty-thousand years ago,
similar sunrise, same tableau:

baffled man, curious dog
huddled around a burning log

as the planet tilts away
toward longer night, shorter day.

Never mind the neighborhood,
helicopter overhead.

Portal of this old frame house
same as a gaping cave mouth.

Similar crows, similar trees,
November killing similar bees.

Mortgage, medical, credit card bills,
nimble deer on distant hills.

Nearby sleeping child and wife,
still the meaning of this life.

Kneelers before their crucifix,
same magicians, similar tricks

as the horned priest knocking bones,
chanting amid the standing stones.

Regardless of how they weep and pray,
mortality's writ in the DNA.

Mausoleums, barrow mounds,
equally bereft of sounds.

Grape on the vine, wine on the tongue,
same human voice when song is sung.

Dreams envisioned on a bed of grass
elusive as those that rise and pass

twitching eyes of urban men.
Mattress, alarm clock, ball point pen

lying in wait to write it all,
same as paintings on a limestone wall.

Baffled man, curious dog,
huddled about a burning log,

long ago and far away,
today, tomorrow, yesterday.

At the Grave of Baudelaire,
Cimetière du Montparnasse

Surely the whores have
long since ceased to
visit this sealed cell

or else ubiquitous crows
cawing in the linden
are those deported

souls, begrimed and
clawed, airborne finally
above the alleys.

The Scars of Gillette, Wyoming

Red rock, dun soil, short-grass prairie
pronghorn own, placid
where they graze and recline, aware

only of wind scent and changing light
rippling across gouged earth, lucid
dreaming, indifferent though never numb.

Moonscape over methane beds, over
black rock the bodies of another epoch.
Those great trenches with their

dark groins and grey-dust berms
aren't their scars, they're ours,
the flesh we feed to furnaces,

the burst and blaze we ignite
with mere switch flicks. The heat
we summon on January nights

has a mouth that chews these plains.
What we burn we breathe, lungs
and landscape marked for tomorrows.

The Frightened Poet

He leans on the rail, he nods his head,
twitches thin tail between balusters.
Well wishers are in short supply and his red

tattoo is healing poorly, a raw cluster
of dull shapes concealed in sleeve's shade.
He still dreams of needlebuzz, a sleep buster.

Papa said wordsmiths may ply a good trade
on some planet but not on this blue, troubled rock.
He leans on the rail, ashamed, afraid,

in need of strong drink, some luck, a book
penned by a madman in a dank apartment,
hero gun-stunned and gutted, hung on a hook.

You really must tell me what you meant
says the sweaty woman, a wasp polishing
her stinger, discolored and much bent.

His mirrored face in the window keeps wishing,
sipping sour white wine from a plastic cup.
Later, all this will require embellishing.

Write as if You Have Something to Say

Write as if you had something to say,
as if the sun were burning a hole in your chest,

rising behind frosted trees on some
October morning, willing to illuminate

even reeking heaps of trash, the backs of
wretched bars where drunks tilt, emptying their

sacks of misery into a common lake.
Write as if you were going to die,

because you are, and write as if you might
live forever and never be held to account

for anything you scribed. Write, write,
and forget the hyenas cackling beyond your

candle's penumbra. Write for broken men
who slept last night beneath the bridge,

only a filthy river to sing them
to and from the boondocks of dreams.

Write for the man in his sleek, black car
who believes in the necessity of cruelty,

who sends back his steak for being too rare
but makes love as if gnawing raw meat.

Write for the cougar high in the tree,
watching the hunter below reload.

Write what you taste, what you hear, give
even the pestering fly its due. Acknowledge

the worm, acknowledge the bulbous
fungus erupting from a fallen spruce.

What use is silence if you are not properly
cloistered, content to noiselessly disperse

when your allotted span of years concludes?
Write in your chilly cell and ignore the matins

bell, the abbot's remonstration, and never
submit to prostrate your pen.

Write as if you were made of unassembled
lightning hidden in a thunderhead riding

high above a forest of tinder-dry pine.
Unleash yourself, knowing you need not aim.

Write now, since there is no other time. Write
whether you want to or not, whether you're

instructed to sit still or ordered to move.
Write what you want to, not what shills insist

will sell. Write as if your tongue were afire,
your hands possessed, your lungs awash in

pure oxygen, your heart in adrenaline.
Pause only briefly at imprecise words,

searching their undersides for concealed
creatures writhing in rich murk. Write longer

than you should, sharper than is fair, explore
the very corners where the light won't shine.

Write as if you had something to say
because if you do, you have.

In a House of Stone

In a house of stone, history
rings, reverberant tones

loosen fictions at their joints,
softening mortar until

walls sag and words like winds
sough in the gaps, ephemeral

cicatrix of frost dripping
to the sill. Who can live

in such a house without one
dull regret to fill up the hole

of his hearth? The pull pull
of illness pocks the smooth

façade and starlings choke forth
pseudo-song from bare elms,

in time with the broom
sweeping shards from stairs.

To dream in a house of stone
you must sleep like the dead,

decomposing visions into
constituent elements, vivid

colors, snippets of speech,
non-sequiturs, the fur and teeth

of strange beasts howling in a
far forest. In the stone kitchen

you must make a meal
of try and fail. Even shadows

in the hall will not conceal
what you said but did not feel.

Colorado Eulogy

Sunlight gilds a
wood floor worn by
many shoes, by
familiar fair winds
and pale, fragrant
hallucinations
chasing troubles
as dusk hangs
darkness on the elms.
Morning will lurk
all night long among
unsprung lilacs
until ready to polish
dents where errant
baseballs bruised
the house's siding,
evenings when music
spilled over the sill and
magpies swooped low.
Such visions flow
past her daughter's shoulder,
she who sits beside
her mother's bed.
Warm still the hand, dim
the sharp moon, secret
these lost scenes
only she sees under
high snowfields July
fails to melt,
slopes she climbed
just to love such a
slow, surreal descent.

Rhiwddolion Rondeau

If the old elms fall, crush the house,
we'll measure our lives in hours,
find gardens where before were none,
sleep away the warm afternoon,
spend a slow night near outer space.

I will ask you to show inner grace
and I'll carry you up the course.
We'll drink red wine in dappled sun
if the old elms fall.

Let us both for pleasure be fierce.
We may yet outrun the hounds,
beside us our daughter and son,
to Rhiwddolion's hills deep green,
cottage beside a watercourse,
if the old elms fall.

Father, When You Died

I crawled in after you, my knees bleeding
from crossing shattered silicon wafers, and then

came the bowling balls, every one you ever
hurled down the slats. They knocked me backward,

a rubber doll tumbling home to live longer.
I heard what you said, don't try to kid me,

buster. I woke up one day to find myself
standing at a blackboard, half-finished sentence

beckoning the fisted chalk. I went home and
held the children tight to my chest. I said prayers

best not to repeat here. The children were anchors
and my arms their two chains. The ocean was insane

with waves. How did you do it, manage to sail
beyond my map's edge until death? Was I as

unimportant then as I have since become?
Who will interpret the complex charts you left

unfinished on your desk? Giant father,
your huge shoes crushed the village I lived in

many times, though I always escaped unharmed.
I know you will surface, a barnacled humpback

off the coast of my unspoken love for you,
aware that I never could swim.

To a Fly, Drowned in Single Malt

Vapors draw down frequent fliers,
down to the liquor's amber fires.

Thermals rising off the malt
coax a grubber in vulgar uglysuit.

Near-empty tumbler lingers, moist,
deep enough to drown a thirsty pest.

Death's expensive if you drink
fine Scottish whisky standing at the sink,

cheap if you eat what others leave,
never pay for drinks and forego all love.

Dive, fly, dive, sip the glossy broth.
Winter has fingers and a mouth.

Time's no friend to either of us—
wait a short while, then ride the bus.

Hush now, listen, grog doesn't lie.
Barleycorn John sings a lullaby.

What Was the Bell I Heard

What was the bell I heard, a cough from
time's throat, a wind again sweeping

dust off the butte, wearing down
redrock smooth and exposed

under November sunrise? What
was the bell I heard, a blue sound

if ever there was, a chime low enough
to soften nightmares, to quiet newborns

who have made their point, now content
to lie still in their fathers' arms,

unaware they are fresh grist between
millstones of earth and sky in an

infinite multiverse? What, after all,
was the bell I heard, a call jackpines

shiver up, illuminated snowy plumes,
spun crystal aloft in clean cold air

that holds the note, harmonizes
with far basso profundo of tumbling

boulders, cores cold as any rock
on any unrecognized moon?

The Crows Who Own the Meadow

The river is a bed of rock,
the water a lover's
tender tongue, a plunge

of tea-tinted snowmelt
frothing in narrow falls as
indigo shadows reclaim the lake

from beneath. Don't argue with crows
who own the meadow, deaf to
human desire and its history

of flightlessness.
Wrestle instead a succubus and if
you lose, lie still, be pain, be the

shredded flesh daybreak
regenerates, trading memory
for silver leaves shivering

in breezes, bruised. If on the trail
the young bull moose refuses to
yield, poses ungulate bones

and lowers a broad velvet rack,
run and hope the forest
falls behind, sudden wind bending

lodgepoles until some tilt and
topple into the supple river,
always spilling and sprinting away.

The Morning of My Release

On the morning of my release I will
escape as a trout slips from the hands
of a starved man who imagined him
gutted and buttered above a sizzling
pan. I will slide into the cool river and
make for the far bank, swim downstream
with the current, fighting nothing.

On the morning of my release, twenty
crows will caw from the cottonwoods,
taunting my captors for failing.
They will follow me home, elm
to ash, mistaken for scavengers,
smarter than angels, friends since
childhood, blackwinged defenders.

On the morning of my release, concrete
will crumble from ceiling and lintel,
great cracks yawning in walls and walks,
but only in dreams, but only in dreams.
Behind my back, a vacuum will suck
my replacement in, the void shuddering
and belching a puff of black smoke.

On the morning of my release I'll walk
north, naked except for a song and
scar tissue, a-thrill with fevered joy.
The fox will acknowledge me at dawn,
both of us hunting to fill a hunger,
both of us roaming and at risk,
both of us finally wild again.

The Last Thing I'll Forget

Scent of her skin on a summer day,
knee deep in Root River shallows.

Crows arguing for a harsher sentence,
insistently just the one word.

Precisely how far the rocky ledge,
as toeholds in ice turn slick.

How a meteor melts, an orange arc
and a bluegreen finishing flash.

Why I Gave Away My Wings

for Ginny

If we must love well just
one thing before the light fades,

let it be earth not air, the body
of the lover not the idea of her

body, the flesh that welcomes
flesh, neither desire nor the captive

bird whose language I'll never
acquire. I gave away my wings

because Daedalus had two sons
but the myth never mentions me.

The fish promised gills but they
lied and I barely made it back

to shore. For decades I practiced
my guitar but never learned to sing.

I spent afternoons in the cherry tree
that refused to fruit until I

climbed back down. I joined the circus
but spent each night selling tickets

outside the tent, the roaring
lions and the whipcrack a tease.

I gave away my wings because,
pressed between pages, I grew

flat and inky, a symbol-shifter never
close to a crow, never swift as a

swallow, never hawk-fierce or
capable of flying in formation.

Better, I found, to be bound
and shelved, to await some distant

opening. I flew as a child but then
one day I awoke and my beak

had become a pair of lips, my bones
were heavy and no longer hollow,

and I fell from my perch and I fell
from my perch again. But as every

flying child knows there's
so much to forgive and regret.

I gave away my wings and learned
to love the body lying beside mine

in the grass. This was worth the loss.
I need never return to the sky.

What the Houseplant Said

In the morning as I make coffee,
my last dream growing transparent
at the edge of vision, I hear the geranium
whisper. Don't think me mad.
I also hear rough words in crows' caws,
songs in the rattle of seedpods.
I feel the limbs of a lover
caress my own in the river,
find signs in bleached coyote bones
splayed at the mouth of a cave,
feel kinship when tall grasses
whip in autumn wind. Sure,
it's a gamble to tell people this,
and that's what the houseplant said.

NOTES

The Antikythera mechanism, a multi-geared bronze device of great complexity, was discovered in 1901 in the ribs of an ancient Roman cargo ship that sank off the coast of Greece around 79 B.C.E. Researchers have deciphered most of the 2,000 characters inscribed on its surface, which suggest it functioned as an analog computer capable of precisely calculating the movements of stellar bodies.

Cahirballykinvarga is an Iron Age ring fort in the Burren, in western Ireland. Although it is much eroded from the passage of several thousand years, it is still a remarkable ruin. Its dry stone walls stand more than five feet thick and 15 feet high, enclosing an oval space more than 150 feet in diameter. A great chevaulx-de-frise forms an outer ring—a field of jumbled stones meant to slow the approach of an enemy on foot or horse. Bless the taciturn farmer, steward of the site, who did his best to misdirect us.

Rhiwddolion [pronounced *roo-TOE-lee-un*] is a remote, abandoned village near Mt. Snowdon in north Wales. It lies along an ancient Roman road, Sarn Helen, whose enormous flagstones are still traversable. For a time it was home to people who worked the nearby slate quarry but now ferns and sheep have claimed the ruined stone huts.

CPSIA information can be obtained at www.ICGtesting.com
Printed in the USA
LVOW11s0103311215

468564LV00004B/58/P